Memoir of a Hero

And Other Poems

By Courtney Morrow

Memoir of a Hero and Other Poems

ISBN: 978-1-105-39774-5

Published by Courtney Morrow, 680 Fall Creek Dr. Unit 2, Branson, MO 65616.

Introduction

The following poems were written when something particular inspired me. Whatever interested me or moved me at the time, I wrote my feelings about it down on paper, keeping the papers all these years.

The subjects range in variation from Branson to the *Titanic* to disaster relief to teenage angst. I tend to write my poems vaguely and let the reader try to understand what it is about. It makes the poem a little more fun when you do not know what it's about. Sometimes, you know exactly what the poet is writing about, and sometimes you make your own translation.

Miscellaneous

The following poems are fun musings about interests in my life; a little something fun to get the ball rolling.

Alone

Look! Up in the sky!
I see the blue bird;
He races among skyscrapers.
He is alone.

Look! Up in the sky!
I see him every day;
He is always saving someone.
He must be alone.

Look! Up in the sky!
Many demand his help;
Many envy the savior.
Truly, he is alone.

Look! Up in the sky!
No one to relate to;
How can they understand?
The super man is alone.

Listen to the Music

The beat of the city perpetuates;
You can hear it throughout the
town.
Even after leaving,
The music of the town can still be
heard.
The singers, the comedians, the
stores—
All a part of its history.
The museums, the parks, the
restaurants—
Everything is full of excitement.
Have you been to the family park
Full of people in 19th century dress?
Have you seen the great Ship of
Dreams
Docked at the main highway?
Have you heard any of the
performers

Whose theatres line the main strip?
Spring is a lovely time to visit,
When the many trees and flowers
    are in bloom.
Summer is beautiful and amazing,
Full of people and things to do.
Autumn is the time when artists
    come together,
Crafting for all around to see.
Christmas is the best of all,
When the whole city lights up at
    night.
There is joy everywhere you look;
You can feel the yuletide spirit in
    the air.
There is never a bad time to travel
    here;
Come and listen to the music.

Winter Wonders

Dazzling, sparkling—
Snow falls from above,
Covering the ground
With a blanket as white as a dove.
Oh, the snow falls like feathers,
And I long to go out,
So I can enjoy the snow
And dance about.
After bounding through the snow,
It's nice to curl up inside
With a warm blanket
And my mother by my side.
She'll wrap her arms around me
And warm me up
As we watch a movie
And drink cocoa in a cup.
Can any sight be better
Than a snowstorm in December,
When lights are shining on the tree

And love is fresh as winter?
This is why winter is great—
Why we long for it all year;
It's just waiting to show us
What it means to have Christmas
    cheer.

Teenage Angst

The following five poems were written during my high school years. At the time, I was very confused and—like all teenagers—angst-ridden. And angst-ridden teenagers that also happen to be writers will write angst-ridden, dark poems.

Invisible

I talk—no one listens
I talk—no one hears
If they would just open up their eyes
and ears
Every day I'm here
But they don't see me
And I just hope and I don't want to
be
Invisible
Can you see me?
Can you save me?
Invisible
This can't be me
And I just want to be
Alive
Every day I see
Attention all around me
But where is the attention meant for
me?

I don't want this life
Can I make it right?
And can I win and can I survive the
night?
Invisible
Can you see me?
Can you save me?
Invisible
This can't be me
And I just want to be
Alive

Chosen

Do you really know me?
I am more than the eye can see
My soul has been chosen
To save the world from these
    demons
God has chosen me
He has given me
A gift of His Spirit
God will stand with me
He will protect me
It's the future—I can see it
Demons cloud my vision
I just can't wait for the next
    premonition
I see shadows move all around my
    world
I'm just one girl
God will protect me
He will love me

I will cast them out in His Name
His Will for me
Is my destiny
And it will always stay the same

Never Fail

I wait out the day
Hoping I will stay
Alive
Every day is a test
To see if I'm the best
Alive
I will never fail
I will never bail
I don't recognize this world that I
walk in
And everybody's talking
About me
They think I don't know
But they're the ones that don't know
About me
I will never fail
Until I sail
To God

The One

I don't know what I should do
Should I tell them or just try to
make it through
If I confide in them, they won't
understand
Because they don't know who I am
I am strong and independent
I am the one who finished last
I am the one who always sees it
through
I am the one they all depend on
I am the one who saves the world
But if they only knew
Sometimes I lie awake at night
And I think about what in my life is
right
I contemplate it and all I feel is pain
But they don't know about my pain

The secrets of my life are too hard
to tell
Sometimes I feel just like an empty
shell
My friends don't know and I can't
share
Sometimes it's just too hard to bear

Stuck

It’s hard to think about my destiny
It’s hard to think about anything but
me
I know I should care
But I’m straining against the glare
Why is this happening to me?
And the people around me cannot
see
And I can’t let them know
They just want to see me glow
The fire burns, and it consumes
And it’s consuming me, too
I try to fight it, but it’s no use
I’m stuck with this abuse
This is slowly killing me
Why can’t they see?
I can’t go on
And I won’t make it until dawn

History

History has been an interest of mine since high school graduation. I love reading about real-life events that happened however many years ago. The following poems range from Columbus to *Titanic* to space exploration to the events of 9/11. History has always had a way of moving me.

Courtney Morrow

First Sight

I stand at the bow,
Staring into the distance.
How I long for first sight in this
endless fog!
There have been signs of land for
days,
But none shows its face.
The ocean is wider than I projected;
Who knows when we will reach our
destination.
As I gaze into the fog,
A darkness seems to form.
I lean forward as it takes shape.
Our first sight of land has come:
Our first glimpse of a New World.

An Iceberg's Tale

It happened on a cold 15th of April,
Nearly a hundred years previously.
All was calm and peaceful;
No breath of wind as far as I could
see.

I was sleeping soundly that night,
Floating somewhere in the North
Atlantic.
I was awakened by three loud
clangs,
And I turned to see a ship so
majestic.

Five hundred yards away was a
giant leviathan,
The largest ship I'd ever seen.
It was heading straight for me,

Its engines pounding like the cogs of
a great machine.

As it drew nearer still, I heard the
engines stop.
They slowly started up once more
As inch by inch, the ship began to
turn,
And the bow swung to port.

I could see that danger was
imminent;
The liner could not escape
And as the starboard hull made
contact;
I heard a terrible scrape.

The iron ship tore pieces of me
loose
As I punctured the metal below the
waterline.

Water would be flooding the
steamer's forward
compartments;
It was only a matter of time.

As the ship brushed alongside me,
Its lines clipped some ice away.
I watched as the ice fell on the
decks;
The only sign that disaster had come
their way.

The ship stopped once it had sailed
past me,
Which was no easy mantle.
As tiny people began scurrying
about the lifeboats,
The engines ceased their losing
battle.

Tiny lifeboats began to lower
themselves
As bright rockets were launched
from the doomed ship.
The bow became submerged as the
people became frantic;
They could now feel the liner's
dreadful tip.

Almost all the lifeboats were gone,
But there were still many to be
rescued.
By now, the bridge was under the
water,
And there was nothing anyone could
do.

As the people hurried towards the
stern,
The boat tilted at a steep angle.

Many people began jumping to
safety,
Watching the crack that had
appeared at the fourth funnel.

The ship split down to the keel;
The stern falling back onto the
water.
It floated for a minute or so
Until the bow began to pull it under.

The broken ship floated for several
moments
And slowly began to go under
As people jumped from the stern
To avoid being pulled under the
water.

Within seconds, the mighty liner
was gone,

With nothing left but screaming,
helpless passengers.
I wondered how long they would
last
Before succumbing to the cold,
frigid waters.

By the time the sun rose on a bleak
scene,
The people in the sea had frozen to
death.
Another ship had arrived for the
survivors;
The scene took away my very
breath.

And now, when asked to recount my
tale,
I tell them of the tragic event that
cold night:

Of how some died nobly and with
honor
As the great Ship of Dreams,
Titanic, went into the sea,
blazing with light.

Till Morning Light

The floor beneath me tilts—
I feel death around me—
And I race for the light.

The water rushes forward,
Waiting to capture me
And make me its own.

Can I survive till morning light?

There is no more help here;
Just screaming souls
As we recognize our dying day.

So much fear
Permeates the night
And drowns us all.

Can I survive till morning light?

Two hours into Monday morning;
I'm on the end of the liner
As it reaches its peak.

I hang on to cold metal
As she stands on her head
In the middle of nowhere.

Can I survive till morning light?

She plunges into darkness;
I feel the pain on my mind—
Cold, cold, cold—never ending.

This soul is not ready;
I beg for mercy
From the heavens.

Can I survive till morning light?

Within ten minutes,
The world goes black.
I will not survive till morning light.

Mankind's Leap

An astronaut opens the outer door of
the lunar lander
And emerges into a foreign world—
An alien landscape much like a
desert of the United States.
The ground sprawls gray and bright
beneath him.
The sky remains as black and
endless as ever.
The astronaut glances up and sees
his home planet Earth—
A mere blue marble in the black
void.
He climbs down the ladder towards
the ground.
As his foot sinks into the fine
powder,
He speaks his famous words:
"That's one small step for man…

One giant leap for mankind."

Successful Failure

The craft bobbed in the water,
Waiting to unload its occupants.
A man inside sat up,
The newfound gravity weighing him
down.
He thought about the journey thus
far,
All still clear in his mind—
The liftoff from the Earth's surface,
The weightlessness in the
vacuumous space,
The explosion that crippled their
craft,
The long journey back to their home
planet—
All leading to the longest four
minutes of his life.
The man looked at his two
crewmen,

Thankful to be alive.
He shook their hands as he keyed
his mic:
"This is Apollo 13, signing off."

Tragedy in September

Two twins stand tall in early
morning,
A symbol of power, prestige and the
American way.
A steel bird hits one—
Smoke and fire billow out.
The second is hit soon after—
More smoke and fire.
People run, people fall, people die.
One twin falls, killing those inside.
The other follows, suffocating the
city with smoke.
Some dead, some trapped, some
free.
The towers once stood tall and
powerful—
Now they lie in ruin, smitten and
weak.

Memoir of a Hero

When we boarded that plane,
We thought it was just another day;
No reason to think
It wouldn't stay that way.

Our flight took to the air
That Tuesday morning,
Heading towards the west
With the forty-four passengers it
was carrying.

None of us was expecting
The yell from four men
That there was a bomb onboard
And they were now the captain.

At the back of the cabin,
We huddled in fear
While we learned of the attacks

Taking place in our country near.

They told us we were headed home,
But their words were just a ruse
As we called loved ones
And heard the horrible news.

One plane had hit the North Tower
Of the World Trade Center.
As the Pentagon was also struck,
A second plane hit the South Tower.

We knew these terrible men
Would not surrender their
  conspiracy
And would use our plane
As a flying bomb—a kamikaze.

No one on the ground
Could solve the problem,
And we would have to devise

A way to disarm them.

We called family and friends
To say goodbye,
Getting ready and prepared
To take back the sky.

When the moment came,
We charged towards the cockpit.
We overpowered them
And took back control of it.

Our plane went down into a field
On that tragic September day.
We gave our hearts and our lives
For our country, the U.S.A.

Hurricane Katrina

These next poems were written for a college poetry assignment, chosen for one specific topic. During high school—and one year after graduation—I went on several volunteer trips down to the Gulf Coast to help survivors of Hurricane Katrina. While helping with disaster relief, I saw many things and heard many amazing stories. And I wanted to share these so everyone could hear.

Hurricane

Wind whipping, soaring, tearing,
    battering—
So fast, so powerful.
Water rushing, flowing, flooding,
    surging—
So deep, so murky.
Debris makes flying missiles—
It's not safe outside.
Houses, stores, trees, people—
All caught in a deadly storm.
Destruction and death all around—
There is nothing left.
Katrina is here.

An Ocean's Swell

The white sand creeps between my
toes,
Cool and soothing in the hot spring
day.
I close my eyes and listen to the
ocean
As it laps the shore in its lazy way.
Sunlight beats down upon my skin,
Warming my body drenched in salt
water.
I lay back against my towel
And take in the day—there never
will be another.
The blue sky shines in the
afternoon,
Sporting not a single cloud of white.
High in the blue vastness of the
atmosphere,

A faint white moon hangs, waiting
for night.
The soft roaring of the tide
Begins to lull me into a false
slumber,
Drowning out the past few days
Of endless work for the hurricane
disaster.
Many beachgoers stumble into the
Gulf waters,
Screaming in delight as they play
Whilst the sun and moon shine
down from above,
Competing for dominance on this
warm day.

Sightseeing

My teacher drove me through
Gulfport,
Taking in the sights of the city.
We were both veterans of the first
trip,
Sightseeing as a treat for me.
We drove to the beach at the Gulf,
Parking to walk in the sand.
We saw carved sculptures by the
road
Made of oak trees that survived the
hurricane on land.
Pelicans, turtles and dolphins
Wound their way around the
weaving tree,
Carved so expertly into the wood—
It was certainly a sight to see.
We walked through the windy day,

The sand so fresh in the early
morning.
Our footprints were the first of the
day,
Imprinting themselves over
everything.
Pelicans ran on their webbed feet
Along the edge of the gulf shore,
Flapping their wings at each other
Before taking flight and beginning
to soar.
When we had gotten our fill,
We piled into the car together,
Heading back to the team at the
church
To finish our work in the hot
weather.

The Volunteer's Life

A volunteer team gathers for a photo
As the last day closes with a glow

The past few days have taken their
toll
On the body, mind and soul

Those who stapled shingles on the
roof of the house
Are sunburned like a barbecued
mouse

Those who taped and mudded the
drywall
Are covered in dust from sanding
the hall

Those who cleared storm debris
from the yards

Are bruised and cut from debris
shards

Despite the hardships and sweat
There was as much happiness as
they could get

They talked with the survivors of
the hurricane
Sharing stories of gladness and pain

There were laughs shared among the
team
Making the time as enjoyable as a
dream

One night, they had time for games
and fun
Giving the teenagers a break when
they were done

A sense of accomplishment
permeates the heat
They've helped another survivor get
back on their feet

Friendship Oak

A sapling begins to mature on
Mississippi sand
As a man named Columbus takes
three ships
And sails to Western land from
Eastern state.
While Europe discovers new land,
The sapling grows during many
hardships
As a new nation rises in turmoil and
hate.
The Friendship Oak stands resolute
in the storm.

A sapling becomes an oak as a
nation engages in war
Against the empire that gave it life
initially,

Trying to become an independent
nation in the West.
A Declaration of Independence is
signed on America's Eastern
shore.
George Washington becomes
President of a newfound country.
A new democracy springs into
existence in a land so blessed.
The Friendship Oak stands resolute
in the storm.

An oak braves the wind, rain and
fury
Bearing down so swiftly from
Katrina's gale,
Tearing apart everything in sight.
Still, the oak does not relent in its
tenacity,
But perseveres through the
tempest's wail—

Through the terror of the morning
    light.
The Friendship Oak stands resolute
    in the storm.

I stand at the base of the oak,
Marveling at the history beneath my
    fingertips—
Five hundred plus years and still as
    beautiful as ever.
The Friendship Oak stands resolute
    in the storm.

Light in Darkness

When faced with terrible tragedy,
Many look at the negative—
The downside, the glass half-
empty—
But we must focus on the good
To endure the bad.
Hurricane Katrina devastated many,
But light can always find its way
through the darkness.
On one Mississippi lawn, a white
cross stands tall.
"He has risen, and so shall we,"
Is written with determination for all
to see.
A song rings out on the radio—
"Hang on! Help is on its way!"[1]
It belts out as the volunteer teams

---

[1] Little River Band's "Help Is On Its Way"

Make their way towards the Gulf
    Coast.
An elderly couple's house remains
    one of the last
To stand in the neighborhood.
"We have a beachfront view now,"
They say with a smile.
As a couple rebuilds their house,
They keep the window that faces the
    beach.
"If it can survive Katrina,
It can survive anything."
Inside a storm-ridden house,
A volunteer team finds a water-
    logged Bible
Whose pages are untouched by
    nature's fury.
Through volunteering for disaster
    relief,
It has become clear—

The only way to survive the
aftermath
Is to rejoice in what we still have.

Bible and Related Stories

This section was chosen as the final one because I wanted to end on a high note. I am, first and foremost, a Christian. Through the years, I have been moved by God and His influence in my life and the stories of the Bible. And, of course, when a writer is moved by something, she picks up her pen.

Boy from the Nile

He gazes at the sea,
Amazed at the width of the water.
He is daunted by his imminent task,
Thinking of all that has happened.
Flies, locusts, boils and darkness,
Water to blood, frogs and firstborn
death.
He thinks of his mission
To free his people from slavery.
He has been called for a purpose—
A purpose that now stares him in the
face.
With his staff in hand, he steps into
the sea.

Blessed Morn

A small boy cries in early morning.
His mother picks him from the
cradle
And holds him in her arms.
The baby stares into the crowd
As he smiles at them.
Two young shepherds kneel by his
cradle,
Showing reverence to this young
King.
Three rich men come forward,
Offering gifts of gold, frankincense
and myrrh—
All gifts befitting a holy child.
The baby falls into deep sleep
As this small group heralds his
birth.
The mother places him into the
feeding trough

As a sheep bleats in the stable.
The baby sleeps on in the humble
manger
As a star shines down from the night
sky.

He Perseveres

The blood soaks through his clothes;
The air stings at the fresh wounds
Like the burn of peroxide.
He perseveres.
His scalp is pierced with thorns
From a crown of humiliation.
His strength has been waned from
    him—
The result of grueling torture.
He perseveres.
Slowly, step by step, he walks down
    the city street,
Carrying the wooden beams—
One vertical, one horizontal—
Upon his shoulder.
The onlookers spit and yell and jeer.
He perseveres.
He pulls his burden towards him—
Knows he must finish his journey.

The soldiers escorting him whip him
In an effort to get him moving,
But it only causes more pain.
He perseveres.
He raises his head to see the hill
That would become his grave.
He winces as fatigue slowly
approaches.
He perseveres.
He reaches his destination just as he
collapses.
They force him onto his beam.
They hammer nails into his palms,
his feet—
He cries out.
He perseveres.
The beams are planted—
The condemned man hangs there.
Each breath drawn is agony.
Hour after hour, life ebbs away.
He perseveres.

He cries out once more—
"Tetelestai"—[2]
His spirit flees this world.
He is placed in a tomb Friday night
Only to have his spirit return
 Sunday morning.
He perseveres.

---

[2] Aramaic for "It is finished"

God Caught Me

I once slipped and fell,
Hitting my head on the concrete
floor.
I was in the hospital for a week.
My parents would be very sad
Had God not caught me.

Incredible Journey

A brown patch of forest
On the edge of a church property,
But appearances can be deceiving,
For this forest holds a special
destiny.

When the trees grow bare
And the air grows cold,
There is a wonderful story
That must be told.

The leaves are cleared,
And the mulch is spread,
The tents built sturdy,
And the lights hung overhead.

Each week is spent rehearsing
As the sets transform at long last,
Taking on an ancient presence

Of a time long since passed.

As the scent of campfire smoke
Fills the winter air,
Characters in Biblical dress
Swarm the forest there.

Families in the woods
Heading to the City of David,
The scribes and Rabbi Mordecai
Copying the Holy Scriptures so
sacred.

The Romans standing sentry
Along the trail in the night,
The Pharisees upholding the law
Of the Jews and what is right.

The Levites traveling to atone
For their sins by sacrificial offering,
The wise men following a star

That will lead them to a great King.

The shepherds tending to their flock
When angels appear with good
news,
The city marketplace buzzing
With shops and items to peruse.

The innkeepers offering no room
Other than their stable small,
Which houses a family meek and
humble,
Yet important above all.

Each part of this seemingly barren
forest
Gives life to the tale of a holy birth.
Adventure awaits on the Journey to
Bethlehem,
The story of how God came to earth.

Changed

A true story

One night I had a dream
That my family had me betrayed
They thought I wasn't a Christian
    and insane
And they locked me away

Two years I had spent in an asylum
Waiting the day I could be set free
They unlocked my cell, let me out
And said I had been cured; I am set
    free

I came home to my family
And they welcomed me with open
    arms
For a week I enjoyed my freedom
Until the asylum director tried to
    work her charm

She came and said I had to go back
My family said they saw no cure
I started to run and hide
I thought I was alone for sure

I came to a house and knocked on
the door
The door opened, and I could see
A loving face in the doorway
Staring back at me

I asked if I could come in,
They granted my request
I entered the house to find
A loving family that would give me
rest

I hid in the house of the kind family,
Hoping I wouldn't be found
Until I looked out the window

And saw my mother, making the
rounds

I explained my situation to the
family
Explained I was innocent, at least
They told me they would help me
That I could hide from “the Beast”

My mother knocked on the door
And a little girl answered it
I hid in the hallway
As the girl stood up to my mother
with wit

My mother inquired if I was there
She said that I wouldn’t be harmed
The girl said no, and my mother
paused
Until she saw my arm

She demanded they send me out
The family could do nothing for me
I stepped out the door
And knew I wouldn't again be free

She started to bring me to the
director
I stopped her and said,
"Why are you doing this?
I'd rather be dead."

I appealed to her common sense
And gave her a smile
She paused and thought
For quite a while

She finally gave in
And realized with her heart
That she had been wrong
From the very start

I awoke the next morning to a dark,
empty room
I pondered the dream all morning
long
But it wasn't until later
That I realized that I was in the
wrong

I realized that I wasn't living like a
Christian
And it scared me that I was living a
sinful life
The dream was a message from God
Telling me to make things right

I cried and cried with all my heart
Until I could cry no more
I prayed a prayer
To ask God to cleanse my heart's
cold core

At that moment, something
    wondrous happened
My soul was filled with the joy of
    God's Word
I said, "You're not getting this soul,
    Satan;
It belongs to the Lord."

So now, my life is filled with peace
My heart filled with Christ's love
    abound
For I was once lost,
But now I am found

Courtney Morrow

www.ingramcontent.com/pod-product-compliance
Ingram Content Group UK Ltd.
Pitfield, Milton Keynes, MK11 3LW, UK
UKHW020219250726
13967UKWH00001B/82
9 781105 397745